PRAISE FOR
CAN'T KEEP A STRAIGHT FACE
AND
WHO CARES IF IT'S A CHOICE?

"Just the kind of good-spirited reading you need at the end of a hard day. Recommend it to everyone who's desperately waiting for the next *Dykes to Watch Out For.*"
Carol Seajay, Feminist Bookstore News

"Thoroughly enjoyable, upbeat and lesbian affirming—Ellen Orleans is an accomplished essayist and fine humorist."
Karen Williams

"If everyone in America reads Ellen Orleans's witty and informative book, Geraldo might soon be out of a job. Buy it!"
Ron Romanovsky and Paul Phillips

"Witty and fun! A must read for all your straight friends. Well... all your straight friends who would read a book with the word 'lesbian' in the title!" *Suzanne Westenhoefer*

"Ellen Orleans is hilarious with her snappy explanations and fancy footwork as she answers once and for all the most inane questions ever asked about gay people. *Who Cares If It's a Choice?* is a must for the time capsule."
Diane DiMassa, creator of HotHead Paisan

"Ellen Orleans and Noreen Stevens make a formidable tag team on the down-and-dirty lesbian humor circuit." *Alison Bechdel*

"This is definitely a 'keep one copy on your desk at work, keep one copy on the back of the toilet' book. Buy it, read it, live it. It's a hoot."—*Labyrinth*, Philadelphia

"She's funny. She doesn't do stand-up, does she? Buy this book so Ellen can stay home and write more." *Kate Clinton*

"Her dial-a-dyke and lesbian TV fantasies are a must for lesbian visionaries." *Sojourner*

ALSO BY
ELLEN ORLEANS

Can't Keep A Straight Face
A Lesbian Looks and Laughs at Life

Who Cares If It's A Choice?
Snappy Answers to 101 Nosy, Intrusive
and Highly Personal Questions About
Lesbians and Gay Men

EDITED BY ELLEN ORLEANS

Boulder Voices
Boulder County Lesbian, Gay and Bisexual
Citizens Tell Their Stories

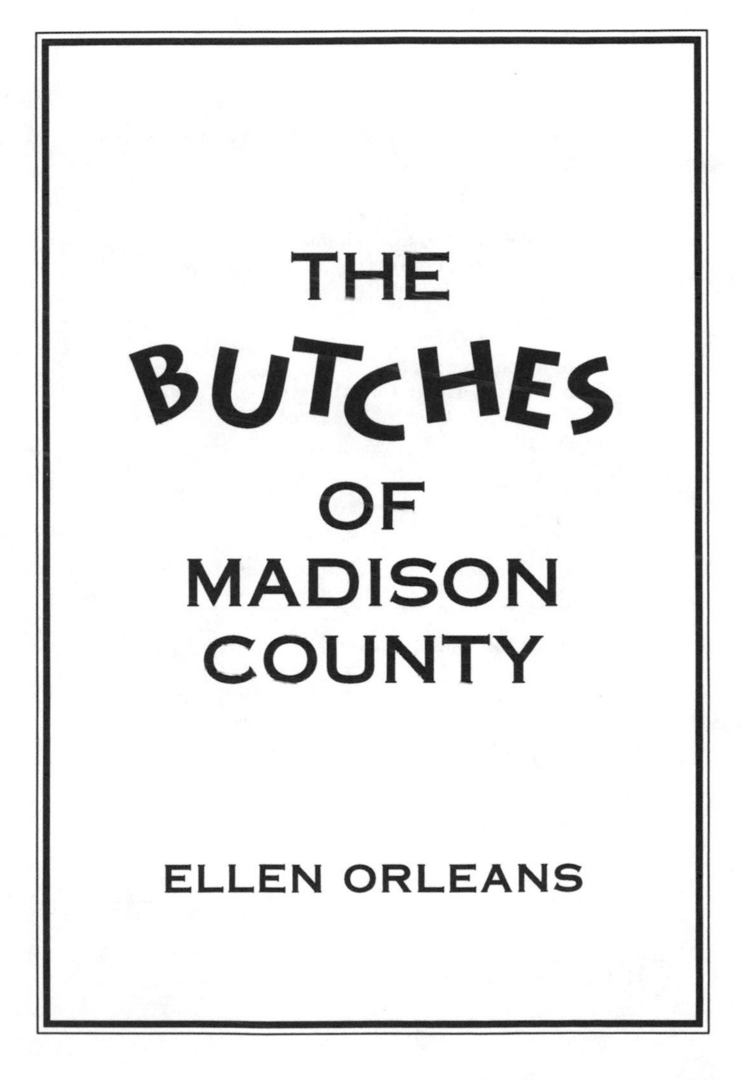

THE BUTCHES OF MADISON COUNTY

ELLEN ORLEANS

For information contact
Rosalind Warren, Laugh Lines Press
P.O. Box 259, Bala Cynwyd, PA 19004
610-668-4252

Printed in U.S.A.
Cover art by Paige Braddock

Library of Congress Catalog Card Number 95-079986

The Butches of Madison County

p. cm

ISBN 0-9632526-6-6

1. Lesbians—Humor
2. Humor—Lesbian Life
3. Fiction—Humor
4. Women—Humor
5. Romance—Lesbians

I. Ellen Orleans, 1961-

For Roz,
who helped me keep
my sense of humor

and

for Laurie
who continues to surprise me

Billie Bold

With a decisive turn of the key, Billie Bold locked the door to her tastefully remodeled turn-of-the-century farmhouse for the last time. Gripping a purple and green duffel bag, she made her way down the flagstone path to the dirt driveway where her forest green Ford Explorer was parked.

A thermos of instant cappuccino and a cooler filled with feta cheese and sun-dried tomato sandwiches were already loaded onto the passenger seat. In the back was a 1974 acoustic guitar, a 1995 PowerBook, a tent, a velvet string bag containing the Mother Peace tarot deck and a small collection of sex toys. There was also, of course, her emergency bad weather kit which included tire chains, a snow shovel, a wool blanket and a box of soggy Saltines. Sure it was the middle of summer and 93°, but you really couldn't be too careful.

Billie got behind the wheel and shut the door. In another lifetime, she would have lit a Lucky Strike but she hadn't lit a cigarette, hadn't inhaled its pungency, encircled herself in the wafting smoke, eyed the puff of smoke from the match as it surrendered to the breath from her lips—anyway, she hadn't smoked in years.

Before backing out the driveway, she mentally inventoried her supply of clothes: one pair of sweat pants, two pairs of jeans, and a pair of multicolored Guatemalan pants that made her feel globally aware. In additional to three new Oxford shirts, she'd packed seven T-shirts, each commemorating a different socially-responsible event—although at present she wore a faded black T-shirt which commemorated nothing.

On her head, she wore her third lover's army cap; on her waist, her fourth lover's leather belt; on her butt, well-worn blue jeans which had belonged to her fifth lover's son.

She glanced again at the back of the Explorer. That was it—her whole life. Except, of course, for what was in the four oversized storage units on the east side of town. Here, though, was the essence, the essentials.

"My rice bowl and sleeping pad," she thought, remembering stories from her week-long retreat at the Duluth Zen Center.

Billie Bold took a final look at the empty house. She'd lived here in Northampton for fifteen years. Here she'd had four lovers, eight roommates, three children (none hers), seven dogs, twelve cats and one iguana. Although not all at the same time.

Although, it often felt that way.

Billie looked at her Casio Pathfinder Triple Sensor watch, which also served as a digital compass, thermometer and altimeter. It was 8:03 am. It was August 5, 1995.

She was fifty years old and it was time to leave.

At the end of the driveway, she clicked her left blinker. There wasn't a car in sight, but she didn't want to get into bad habits. "Visualize Using Your Turn Signal" was her favorite bumper sticker.

Billie pushed "PLAY" on the CD player. Strains of Yanni filled the Explorer. Normally, she would have chosen something upbeat, but today she was in an introspective mood. This was not just another car trip; this was a journey. A journey, although she didn't know it at the time, that would change her life.

Highway Construction on Life's Spiritual Path

Driving through the Holyoke mountains, Billie fiddled with the radio, trying to tune in *A Prairie Home Companion*, or as LaNell, her eleventh lover, liked to call it, *A Hairy Prone Companion*.

Having no luck, Billie flipped off the radio and flexed her back. For the thousandth time she wished she'd gotten herself a cat. A lithe tabby, perhaps, or maybe a squarely-built gray. A cat that would wrap herself around Billie's neck or ride on her shoulder. A cat that would have enough self-esteem to be independent yet enough sensitivity to curl up with Billie when Billie wanted her.

"A cat?" Billie thought to herself. "Hell, that's what I want in a lover."

She sighed. "The absence of an enduring intimacy has plagued me my whole life," she said to the passing road signs.

"Enduring intimacy," she repeated, flipping open a pad of recycled paper with her right hand and jotting down the phrase with her left.

Billie had always loved words. Ever since she was a kid, she'd written down bits of stories and parts of poems on spiral-bound notebooks. Some years ago, she'd shown those notebooks to Sylvia, her irresponsible twelfth lover, who was also a psychotherapist. Instead of being amused as her other lovers had been, Sylvia wondered if there wasn't some sort of obsessive neurosis at play. Billie never bothered showing them to her thirteenth lover.

As Billie contemplated her past, the words of her yoga instructor came to her: *Be Here Now*.

"Be here now." Billie intoned, breathing from her lower belly. But even as she repeated this mantra, she found herself slipping Ferron's *Driver* into the CD player and setting the cruise control, her mind drifting backward in time.

"Screw it," Billie said. "I'll be here now, later."

A Member of the Family

Billie hadn't been a very good child—that is, she hadn't been a very childlike child. The illegitimate offspring of a combat photographer and a Pacific Army nurse, she took refuge in her dreams of becoming a famous writer.

As a teenager, Billie was enthralled with Emily Dickinson, composing mournful poems for the school newspaper. By high school, Dorothy Parker was her idol and Billie wanted a career as a writer.

Her mother ridiculed her dreams. "Marry a hard-working man," she admonished. "Doesn't matter if he's dull, as long as he can support you."

Halfway through Billie's senior year, a new girl, Corey, showed up in class. Already nineteen, Corey had been thrown out of several private girls' schools. Billie was impressed and they became friends.

Walking home one day through a new subdivision, Corey pulled Billie up the stairs of a house under construction.

"You can still see the sky," Billie said, peering through the wooden beams.

"Look over here," Corey said and when Billie turned, Corey kissed her on the mouth. The kiss so thoroughly filled each crevice of Billie's body that it took a moment for her to register that it had come from female lips and she wasn't *supposed* to feel good.

Billie spent the next four months in a mix of remorse and delight: she was thrilled to be doing something so "wrong," relieved to learn it was just a phase, while at the same time determined to relish each moment before this phase passed.

That summer Billie and Corey got jobs as counselors at Corey's uncle's camp in New York State. The job changed Billie's life. It wasn't the canoeing, the batiking or singing *Leaving on a Jet Plane* —it was the weekend escapes to an Oswego bar where Corey introduced her to "the life."

The bar both fascinated and scared Billie with its smoking, drinking and cross-dressing. But the worst part for Billie was that she couldn't figure out if she was butch or femme. If she slicked her hair back with VO-5, she looked like a prepubescent version of Sal Mineo. Teasing it into a bouffant was no better—she felt like a ditzy extra from *Bye Bye Birdie.*

"I'm a mutant lesbian," Billie fretted as she slinked into the darkest booth in the bar, bumping right into two women making out. And that's how she met Foxie and Mamie.

Foxie and Mamie took Billie in. They answered her questions—*Is being a lesbian legal?* (Sometimes) and

Should I tell my mother? (No)—and introduced her to another butch/femme couple, B.J. and Charlie. The five of them swapped stories and shared secrets. She learned that Charlie was half-Negro, (or "Black" as B.J. had corrected her) and that B.J. was Jewish (the first Jew Billie had ever met). It all felt terribly mature, especially when B.J. taught Billie to blow smoke rings. Together, they became the family Billie felt she'd never had.

After the summer, Corey split for Boston but Billie stayed on. By the following spring, though, Billie became restless. She bought a VW bug (a purchase that granted her full-fledged membership in the lesbian nation) and took off for San Francisco, where she watched the summer of love unfold around her. In Golden Gate park, she watched girls make love to each other, but she wondered where all the butches were. When she dared to ask, the response was usually scorn or stoned laughter, although one woman did suggest Los Angeles.

Two years later, she called it quits. Packing up her faithful Bug for the return trip, she said to herself, "I'm 23 years old already; it's time to get on with my life."

Blazer Dyke

Billie, the now 50-year-old Billie, pulled into a rest area for a bathroom break and—to the surprise of the other motorists—to practice her *t'ai chi* between picnic tables.

Back in the Explorer, Billie thought about the years after San Francisco. Enrolling at Barnard, she'd fallen in love often, following lovers to exotic locales: a cabin near the Puget Sound, a commune in the Blue Ridge Mountains, a fourth floor walk-up on Staten Island.

After meeting Marta, a CPA, Billie went upscale. She bought six bolo ties, began an accounting course, and traded the ancient Bug for a Honda Civic. For a while, she even edited a newsletter for a stuffy lesbian networking group. But after producing an April Fool's edition proclaiming: *"Dip Me in Money and Throw Me to the Lesbians!"* Billie was asked to leave.

When Marta left the relationship—moving to New Mexico to enroll in an acupuncture program—Billie had a broken heart, but also a healthy bank account. She bought a rambling farmhouse, upgraded to an Accord and went back to school for her Masters in Psychology.

There she met Sylvia, a former public relations consultant who helped Billie convert the house into Sappho Heights Healing Retreat. The night of Billie's graduation, when Sylvia and Billie did some personal healing of their own in the newly-installed hot tub, they became more than just business partners.

Then Marta returned from the Southwest, having sold her "Vision Quests for White People" franchise to a Swiss woman, Inga Leaping Deer. Like a good lesbian, Billie made peace with her ex. Sylvia, also in proper dyke fashion, accepted Marta into the fold, and even hired her to do payroll for her latest venture, Java Jitters: An Espresso Bar.

As fate would have it, Marta and Sylvia fell in love over a Lotus spreadsheet. Stunned, Billie remodeled Sappho Heights into a Bed and Breakfast. Closeted yet affluent dykes came pouring in. To compensate for her gross capitalism, Billie ran free "Femmes over Forty" support groups.

"But what good is money without the love of a soulmate?" Billie thought. She was now an hour past Cleveland, speeding west on I-80 towards. . . where? It didn't matter that she'd earned her Master's degree, meditated seven hours a week or survived menopause: she still felt empty.

With a sudden sadness, it all became clear to Billie. Her life was as shallow as a Hollywood movie, as trivial as a paperback romance. "Billie Bold," she said to herself, "you're nothing but a lesbian cliché."

Patsy Plain

As Billie Bold zoomed across the Interstate, bemoaning her clichédom, hundreds of miles to the west a comely but exhausted farm wife swung listlessly on a porch swing. Thirty-nine-year-old Patsy Oakshire Plain shook her head.

"I guess it's time to admit that a simple day's repairs like rerouting the irrigation pipes, sharpening the lawn mower blades and reroofing the dog house just plain takes it out of me," she thought to herself.

Upstairs, her husband and daughter were packing for a 5-day trip to Normal, Illinois. He was off to an Organic Root Vegetable Growers conference, she to visit a college friend.

Staring into the distance, Patsy sighed—again she had the feeling that something had gone drastically wrong in her life. Here she was, the mother of an ever more distant teenager and the wife of an increasingly introverted—no, be honest, eccentric—organic carrot growing husband. How had this happened?

Michael. Michael was the missing piece. In high school, Patsy and Michael had been inseparable. A perfect gentleman, Michael liked to talk about art, not football; music, not pickup trucks. Best of all, he was never pushy about sex.

During their senior year, Patsy and Michael went to Chicago to visit the Art Institute and see theater. It was a week Patsy never forgot; twenty-five years later, it still stood out like a shining precious gem on the slag heap of life.

So why had Michael (never "Mike") suddenly taken off, just as they were graduating and planning to marry? And why to San Francisco of all places? Eventually, Patsy received a postcard from him: Michael was living in a place called "The Castro." Odd, thought Patsy, who'd never imagined he was a Communist.

Michael's scraggly-bearded brother Pete returned from Canada in March. For lack of anything better to do, Patsy spent time with him. Pete was mildly interesting—a diversion until she left for college.

When Pete proposed to her, Patsy, pressured by family expectations as well as her incredibly low self-esteem, reluctantly agreed. On their wedding night, Pete passed out in the heart shaped tub in their honeymoon hotel. Patsy, more relieved than disappointed, read *Fear of Flying* until midnight then fell asleep dreaming of Michael, who'd sent a brief note with his regrets and a large color book of Michaelangelo's work.

For the next two years, while Pete pursued his dream of organic carrot farming, Patsy learned to do everything else: cook the meals, clean the gutters, feed the chickens, fix dripping faucets, plaster the cracks in the bedroom wall. Everything, it seemed, but neuter the family dog.

When Pete's rubber broke in the back seat of their Plymouth Duster on a spontaneous excursion to Inspiration Point, Patsy knew she'd become pregnant. She was delighted. Pete didn't want to bring kids into this sick, dangerous world, but Patsy wanted company; no, more than that, she wanted a reason to exist. Pete had his organic carrots (he refused to increase his line to any other vegetable, saying he wanted to fully explore all the possibilities of carrots before moving on to, say, beets, turnips or, dare he say it, the squash families), but Patsy had no one.

Their daughter arrived in the bicentennial year. Pete insisted that they name her Peace, as a message to the nation. Patsy wanted a second child, but Pete was adamant. He settled the matter by treating himself to a vasectomy for his 30th birthday.

The years went on. Patsy was a girl scout troop leader, headed the civic covered bridge restoration project, worked on and off at her parents' store, ran the house and cared for the chickens, barn cats and Pete's dogs, a series of chocolate Labradors all named Prince.

But now, on this muggy evening, Patsy felt she had nothing to show for herself but a moody daughter and a needy husband—her days reduced to a sluggish stream of tiresome details in a life she'd never wanted.

Still, she did have the week to herself. And although she imagined it would pass pleasantly enough, she was sure it would be about as exciting as her last name.

The Heartland

As Patsy waved good-bye to her daughter and husband on Sunday morning, Billie Bold was checking out of her motel room. Heading for the Interstate, she knew she'd soon be over the Indiana border, facing a big temptation. Despite herself, Billie fantasized about Highway 69 which ran north to Michigan, fantasized about the herds of naked torsos and smorgasbord of pleasures that awaited her just beyond the festival gate.

Then she berated herself. "There you go again, thinking with your G-spot." No, she would not waiver from her three year commitment to celibacy and personal growth.

And how she had grown. Working through her *Creative Catharsis* workbook, Billie had rediscovered her inner writer. Billie had also immersed herself in relationship books: *The Dance of Anger, The Dance of Intimacy, The Dance of Ennui.*

As the off-ramp to Michigan loomed, Billie cried out "Therapist, heal thyself!" And with this empowering affirmation, she shot past Highway 69. No, the Music Festival wasn't what she needed. What she needed lay in Iowa.

Why Iowa? Four reasons: Foxie, Mamie, Charlie and B.J. For, as Billie had continued her personal growth work, she'd come to understand that the best time of her life had been that year in Oswego.

So, eight months ago she'd begun calling around, trying to track down these friends of her youth. Finally, she got word from Corey herself, now an analyst with Merrill Lynch.

"The four of them have all bought land, in—get this—Iowa. I couldn't get a phone number for Charlie and B.J., and Foxie and Mamie have refused to get an answering machine, so good luck getting in touch."

So, Billie was going to Iowa. And not just to any part of Iowa, but to Madison County, where she would reconnect with the spirit of her incipient lesbian years, reclaim her womynity, unleash her cosmic fire and write about it all in the process.

Shortly after two o'clock, she checked into The Covered Bridges Motel, picked up the phone and dialed Foxie and Mamie's number.

As she listened to it ring on the other end, Billie was gripped with momentary panic. What if Foxie and Mamie had become exquisitely rich and were vacationing in France? Or had become Buddhists and were traveling in Tibet? What if this was no longer their phone number at all but that of a cheerful, blond-haired couple with four kids who'd turned their lives over to Jesus and hated gay people?

"Hello," a hearty voice boomed.

"Hello. I'm trying to reach Foxie or Mamie."

"Well, you got Mamie."

"Mamie, this is Billie. Billie Bold. From Oswego? "

"Billie!" she pulled the receiver away from her mouth, "Foxie, you'll never guess who's on the phone."

"Foxie? Is Foxie there with you?"

"Course she is." Mamie laughed her throaty, smoker's laugh.

Tears welled in Billie's eyes. "I want to visit you and talk to you and write about your lives—as part of my personal journey and for future generations too."

"Slow down, girl. Where *are* you? In Winterset? No kidding. Of course drop in. We're always here. Unless we're out, but if we are, we'll be back."

Billie scribbled down a cumbersome set of directions. A half hour later, she was driving in circles, bouncing on dusty roads, hopelessly lost. Passing a farmhouse, she slowed the Explorer. A hand painted mailbox read:

The Plains
Pete, Patsy, Peace and Prince

As she neared the house, she saw a woman sitting on the porch swing. She wore faded cut offs and a cotton shirt. She was wholesome, yet stunning, like a Gap ad—no, a Calvin Klein ad. As the woman rose and walked toward her, Billie suddenly had a feeling that her three years of self-imposed celibacy were about to end ahead of schedule.

A Distant Muffler

The porch swing creaked as Patsy sat down, but she didn't jump up for the WD-40 as she normally would have.

"This is my vacation," Patsy reminded herself, sipping from her glass of unfiltered, lukewarm tap water.

Gazing at the lightly swaying grasses in front of her, Patsy heard a car slow, then head down the gravel drive towards the house.

Wiping the sweat off her forehead, Patsy stood up and walked toward the sound. Another day, she might have slipped into the kitchen until the car disappeared. Or pulled out the family shot gun and scared the car off.

But today was not other days. Today Patsy Plain felt curious. Today, she wanted an adventure.

Explorers

It wasn't a car, it turned out, but one of those all-terrain sport utility vehicles that was something between a van and a truck. The door opened and Patsy's life changed forever.

Out stepped a woman the likes of whom Patsy had never seen. Elegant yet sturdy, the woman wore tan trousers, carefully ironed, yet somehow loose and casual too. A smart and colorful belt met a crisply-pressed white cotton shirt, its rolled up sleeves revealing well-muscled forearms. The stranger's broad shoulders were confident and her jawline pronounced yet not harsh, her breasts large yet . . . breasts? Patsy had never examined another woman's *breasts* before.

Shaking off the image, Patsy thought, "If someone published an oversized coffee table book entitled *Intriguing Women of North America*, then this woman, this vision of confidence and purpose, would surely be on the cover."

The woman turned and smiled. "Uh, I'm wondering

if you could help me. I'm looking for—" she paused momentarily, "Bull Dyke Ranch."

Patsy knew that she could have been in many other places at this moment: at the video shop in town, out back at the compost pile, stuck on the phone with a guy selling carpet cleaning. She could have been there and not here and the Explorer would have driven by, cast to the winds of chance. Not unlike the unbridled fluff of the milkweed pod, not unlike. . . .

Patsy heard the woman clearing her throat and emerged from her pondering. "Bull Dyke Ranch? It's not far from here."

Then Patsy did something she hadn't done in many, many years. She asserted herself. "I can show you where it is," she said.

Patsy never knew what caused her to be so forward that day. Maybe it was the sudden freedom of having the house to herself, maybe it was a subtle yet compelling energy emanating from this woman, or perhaps, just perhaps it was that she'd always wanted to get a look inside one of those sport utility vehicles.

"That would be terrific," said Billie, her voice brimming with warmth and self-composure. Patsy decided she was in the presence of greatness.

So, Patsy, having in that simple moment become a surfer on the wave of decisiveness, a hang glider on the winds of action, yes, a willing pilgrim on the cosmic whoosh of chance, walked toward the Explorer.

"Just need to clear off some space," Billie said, shifting the brightly colored thermos and cooler to the back of the Explorer. Patsy admired how clean and organized the car was. Pete never bothered to clear his trash out of the beat-up Chevy truck they shared; gas receipts, pop bottles and mis-folded maps littered the muddy floor mats.

Patsy climbed into the passenger seat and watched Billie swing into the driver's side. This stranger moved so deftly, so assuredly. Why Patsy would have called it "an animal-like grace," but then she thought of all those clumsy, gawky animals like rhinos and hippos and the whole pachyderm order in general and suddenly that description seemed ludicrous.

When they reached the end of the drive, Patsy directed Billie to turn left, watching Billie's nicely-shaped fingers grip the steering wheel, her nicely-muscled arms shift the stick, her nicely-styled canvas hiking boots move from break to gas to break again.

"I bet those shoes have seen a lot of miles," Patsy said, her voice brimming with admiration.

"Actually, I ordered them from Eddie Bauer's just last month," Billie said, gazing intently ahead, "but thanks for the thought."

Billie reached into a cleverly-concealed compartment between the seats and pulled out a business card. The purple and black ink on bright white read: Billie Bold, Writer and Chronicler. Below the post office box address was a voice mail number, a cellular phone number, a pager number, a fax number and an e-mail address.

"You're a writer," Patsy exclaimed, "That explains the mystical, god-like qualities I've been sensing." She settled back into her seat, smiling.

"Well," Billie said, "I don't know about—uh—" she cleared her throat, "god-like, but there is a certain mystery to words, an unconscious connection as we transform our hopes, dreams and fears into mere letters of the alphabet. Of course, I've only been a writer for the last two days. And I haven't actually, uh, written anything yet."

Patsy didn't care. She was totally enthralled. "So, are you writing about Bull Dyke Ranch?"

"Why, yes," Billie said, then ventured, "know anything about it?"

"I've seen the sign dozens of time. Always figured it had something to do with livestock irrigation."

Billie shot her a quick look; no, this woman wasn't joking. "Friends of mine live there," she explained. Then nonchalantly outing her old cohorts, she added, "I'm going to interview them about their place in lesbian history." Billie paused. "I hope that doesn't shock you."

Patsy shrugged. "That the women who live at Bull Dyke Ranch are lesbians? Everyone knows that. Lesbians into livestock irrigation." But then Patsy hesitated, "Wait. Are you trying to telling me that *you're* a lesbian too? Or are you just doing research for Public Radio?"

"I wasn't trying to tell you that in particular, but, as a matter of fact, yes I am."

"No kidding?" Patsy grew visibly excited. "I mean I've seen pictures of you all in *Newsweek* and of course on *Oprah*, but for real? I'll be." Patsy grinned, lightly punching the dash. "I knew there was something special about you."

Then she sat up abruptly.

"What's the matter?" asked Billie, braking slightly.

"The turn. I forgot to tell you to turn back there. But that's okay, you can cut around in a minute. Say, you haven't ever *been* on *Oprah*, have you?"

Caught up in an avid, if one-sided, discussion about lesbians and daytime T.V., Patsy again forgot to cue Billie on an upcoming turn, forcing her to backtrack, then get caught at a railroad crossing. The talk turned to lesbian motherhood.

Once they began moving again, Patsy grew quiet, examining the carpet, contour seats and side panels. "Can I ask you a personal question?" she said at last.

"Here it comes," thought Billie, placing bets in her head. "It's either going to be, 'When did you first know you were gay?' 'Do you think you were born that way?' or the perennial favorite, 'Just what do two women do in bed anyway?'"

"Go ahead," Billie said, bracing herself.

"What do you call this?"

"This?" thought Billie. She had never thought of her homosexuality as a "this." "Usually I call myself a lesbian, sometimes 'dyke.' To the Chamber of Commerce—gay woman. Of course there's also queer, homo, lezzie, sapphist, woman-loving-woman and woman-identified-woman, with their appropriate spelling permutations, of course."

Patsy was amused. "What I meant was, what do you call this thing we're driving in? Do you call it a car or a truck or a van or do you say, 'Honey, I'm taking the sport utility vehicle to the store—want anything?'"

"Oh," Billie said, embarrassed. "Uh, I usually just call it the Explorer. Although, well. . . ." She hesitated, not sure if she should divulge what was still for her a private matter.

"Go on," Patsy said, sensing a secret, and wanting to be in on the fun.

"I sometimes call her—it—Janeway. From *Voyager*."

"*Voyager*? I thought this was an Explorer."

Billie sighed. "*Voyager* is a T.V. show about a starship called Voyager. Janeway is Voyager's female captain. Now, *originally* I considered buying a Voyager—the van that is—just for the name, but that seemed silly. Then I thought of calling the Explorer 'Voyager,' but that was confusing, so I named her Janeway instead."

"I see," said Patsy, more mystified than ever.

They arrived at the gate to Bull Dyke Ranch a half hour later. They both got out of the Explorer, stretched and looked around. "It's too late to drop in now," Billie said, "but I think I'll be able to find my way back tomorrow." She strolled down the shoulder of the dirt road and returned holding a bouquet of Queen Anne's lace, bachelor's buttons and wild pansies.

"For you," Billie said, "for being my navigator."

Patsy was taken aback. It had been years since she'd been given flowers. Pete felt it was wrong to seize live plants from the wild and force them to live the rest of their short lives indoors.

Taking the bouquet from Billie, Patsy realized she'd never gotten flowers from a woman. But oddly enough, she wasn't embarrassed, horrified or aghast. Oddly enough, she found herself—well—quite flattered.

Girl Talk

It only took five minutes to get back home.

As Billie pulled into the driveway, Patsy realized she was not ready to let go of this strange and wonderful woman with the meticulously packed car.

"It's still hot," she ventured. "Would you like a cold drink?"

"If it's not too much trouble," Billie said, "but I don't think you've actually told me your name. You're Patsy of Peter, Patsy, Peace and Prince. Am I right?"

"Yes. Pete is my husband." Did she see a slight drop in Billie's face? "And Peace is my daughter, except no one but Pete calls her that, everyone calls her Oak. And Prince is the dog."

Soon they were sitting at the kitchen table, drinking iced coffee. Patsy tried to be subtle as she stared at Billie's throat muscles downing the cool, caffeinated beverage. Billie wiped her damp brow and asked for another glass.

As she poured in half-and-half, Billie remarked,

"After all these years, I still love to watch the whiteness swirl and eddy through the coffee, like a dance of yin and yang. The beauty is in the contrast, you know."

Patsy knew she'd never look at coffee the same way. Were all lesbians so lyrical? she wondered.

"Are all lesbians so lyrical?" Oh, God, she'd said it out loud.

Billie blushed, but Patsy went on anyway. "I feel silly saying it, but honestly, I pictured lesbians as over-sexed, slightly dangerous women on the prowl. But you aren't like that at all. You're sweet. And I don't feel I have to defend my heterosexuality to you."

Billie laughed. "Damn and here I was hoping—despite my three year pledge of celibacy—that you had fantasies about jumping into bed with me."

Patsy was shocked. But not about the hopping in bed part. "You've taken a three year pledge of celibacy?" she asked, reaching for the Mr. Coffee carafe, "Why?"

"I'm currently working on developing a relationship with *myself,*" Billie grinned. "But don't worry, you'd be safe anyway. I swore off straight women and married women after my short-lived yet thoroughly disastrous thirteenth and fourteenth relationships. "

"With straight and married women?"

"Yes. One of each."

Patsy gave a melodramatic sigh. "No need, then, for me to be worrying about suppressed homosexual urges emerging from *my* libido. Clearly, you aren't interested in taking advantage of my confused, vulnerable state. So, you want to stay for supper?"

Billie chuckled. Patsy sure was gutsy for a farmer's

wife. "Supper? I'd love to. But first I have to get some things out of Janeway, then spend a few minutes making sure everything stays meticulously arranged." Billie smiled at her own obsessiveness. She had a wonderful smile. Patsy could just imagine those teeth nibbling on one of those numbered lovers.

"Billie? About dinner, I, uh, I don't have much normal food." She opened the refrigerator door. " Wait, is a frozen pepperoni pizza okay?"

"Perfect." Billie said, then added, "I *was* wheat-free when I was with my fifth lover, Wildfire, then off dairy after April, my eighth lover, left and of course I've been vegetarian on and off since the 70's. But at this particular point in my life, a frozen pizza with pepperoni would hit the spot."

While the pizza baked, Patsy went upstairs to shower. She found herself humming under the cool water and realized that she had not been this happy in a long time.

Patsy toweled off, then in a brash and shameless move, reached deep into the dresser drawer and took out a pair of *black* underpants. Secretly thrilled to be wearing such a brazen undergarment, Patsy pulled a pair of blue jeans over them, then put on an oversized white T-shirt Oak that had given her for Mother's Day.

As she walked downstairs, Patsy saw Billie washing up in the kitchen sink, using a scrubbie under her nails. Embarrassed, she said, "There's a downstairs bathroom. You're welcome to use it."

"Thanks. I didn't want to be too forward. Besides," Billie said, pausing for effect, "I've washed up under far rougher conditions—under spigots at Michigan, out of my canteen at the Albuquerque Festival, with bottled Evian at the Gulf Coast festival . . . ." She dried her hands with the dish towel.

Patsy had no idea what Billie was talking about. Nonetheless she found herself again filled with girlish admiration. Oblivious, Billie turned to the cooler she'd brought in and pulled out two bottles of Jane Addam's ale. Before Patsy could give her a bottle opener, Billie was wielding a Swiss Army knife with a practiced hand, expertly flicking open the bottles.

Well, not quite expertly. One of the bottle tops landed in Prince's water dish—and when Patsy bent down to fish it out, she noticed that it said "TWIST OFF CAP." But she kept quiet, not wanting to spoil the moment.

"To Madison County," Billie said, raising her bottle in a toast.

Patsy, who had difficulty knowing what to say at intimate moments, was saved by the smell of burning mozzarella wafting from the oven. She quickly clinked her beer bottle, then turned away to investigate.

Dinner Conversation

"Some cheese dripped onto the burner, but the pizza's fine." Patsy closed the oven door and, still uncomfortable at the brief intimacy, said "I think I'll put together a salad."

"Need a hand?" Billie offered.

"No, I'll be just a minute." She walked past Billie, wondering if the older woman was watching her as she walked toward her vegetable garden, where she grew tomatoes, peas, lettuce, herbs—every kind of vegetable, in fact, except carrots.

Patsy had guessed well; Billie *was* looking at her. Watching the way the loose cut of her T-shirt revealed then concealed the shape her back, the curve of her stomach, the edge of her breasts. Billie felt the familiar ache of attraction and wondered if she should struggle against the feelings or quietly enjoy them.

Certainly, she shouldn't act on them. Sure, it was fun to flirt a little, but no more than that. There was her celibacy pledge to think about, but more than that, who wanted to be rejected by a straight, married woman from rural Iowa?

There'd be rumors enough, Billie imagined. Tomorrow, straight, married Patsy would be gossiping with her straight, married friends, telling them how she entertained a lesbian—yes, a real East Coast *lesbian*—who had stumbled onto her farm house looking for directions. She might or might not tell her farmer husband Pete, and if she did, they'd probably just use the experience as fuel for sexual play. Billie shivered, trying to purge the image from her head.

Yet when Patsy entered the kitchen with her colander of fresh-picked produce, and the two of them began rinsing and chopping together, Billie's emotional detachment weakened. Damn! Kitchen chores always made her yearn for domestic fulfillment.

Unbeknownst to Billie, Patsy was experiencing similar feelings. "How wonderful," she thought, "to share the preparation of a meal with someone else."

Over the last few years, Pete had taken to spending hours in front of the computer, talking on the Internet. He couldn't string together two sentences to say to his wife, but he could chat for hours with faceless strangers with made-up names.

Again, the smell of singed cheese interrupted Patsy's ruminations, but Billie was already pulling the pizza out of the oven. "Just a little charred around the edge," she reported.

Patsy brought the pizza, salad and beers to the square maple table she'd stripped, sanded and refinished last summer. Patsy sat down at one end, Billie catty-corner from her. The nervous intimacy returned.

"So," Patsy began, "I noticed you have a guitar with you. Do you play much?"

"I dabble a little. Inherited the damn thing when my sixth lover, Wendy, left Vermont for Arkansas." Billie munched on her salad.

"Your *sixth* lover." Patsy said, trying to keep the conversation moving. "And what number were you up to before you decided to go celibate?"

"Fifteen." Billie helped herself to another slice.

Patsy resumed eating, wondering if fifteen was the average number of lovers for 50-year-old lesbians.

Billie finished her beer then said, "I'm sorry. I'm not keeping up my end of the conversation. You see, I tend to ramble. This evening, this meal—how do I explain—well, it feels almost sacred. I don't want to wreck it."

"Wreck it? By talking?" Patsy asked, aghast. "In this house, I ache for decent conversation."

"Really?" Billie asked.

"Really," Patsy assured her. "Please, tell me about yourself."

Billie looked as happy as Susie Bright in a dildo shop. She burst out, "In the past few days, as I've trekked across these highways of America, I've had time to reflect on my haphazard life and now I look back—" Billie's burst of words trickled down to an introspective drip, "and it all feels like a joke."

Patsy had the urge to reach over and hug Billie, but she didn't know the etiquette around hugging lesbians. Was there a gay Miss Manners? She let Billie continue.

"Driving through Ohio, I said to myself, 'Okay

Billie, so you're the only dyke on earth who hasn't found her place on the lesbian continuum. So what?' I swore I'd rise above it. Bc proud to be the last lesbian stereotype, nobly wandering across America. But," Billie faltered, "now I don't know."

What she couldn't tell Patsy was how this humble Iowa kitchen had brought back that ever-present need for family, for roots. "But what about you?" Billie asked. "What about your life?"

Patsy smiled weakly. "I don't want to sound ungrateful. I have a wonderful daughter, the farm has survived, Pete isn't a raging alcoholic. It's just that I'd like. . ."

"More." Billie finished Patsy's sentence for her, sensing that some intimate boundary had just been crossed. "I know, because I do too."

Red Sky, Purple Shadows

As Billie stacked the plates in the dishwasher, Patsy wondered if she would simply thank her for the meal and be on her way. On her way to an author's adventures, leaving Patsy with only an odd sweet memory of a hot August day.

But then Billie asked, "Join me for an evening stroll?" and Patsy's heart leapt with joy.

Accompanied by Prince, they walked past the porch swing and down the wooden steps. As they moved across the field, the grass grew taller and the sun sunk lower. Billie threw a stick for Prince, but he ignored it.

"Do you walk out here often?" Billie asked.

"We used to," Patsy said, "when Pete and I were first married. But we'd end up talking about alternative irrigation methods or Pete's latest discovery in organic fertilizers, when what I wanted was. . . poetry."

"Poetry," Billie repeated. She leaned against the trunk of an old cottonwood, looked into Patsy's eyes, and quoted:

> Under the sky
> summer red
> and screaming for the moon,
> I ache for the purple shadows
> to come and fill my heart.

"That's, that's beautiful," said Patsy, her voice trembling slightly. "Is it Yeats, Whitman? No, wait. *You* wrote it, didn't you? Penned it on a summer's night like this one, when the world filled you with the quiet tragedy of human mortality."

"Actually, I made the poem—" began Billie.

"Oh, yes, 'made' not 'wrote.' I understand!" cried Patsy. "Crafted it with more than a mere writing utensil, but with your whole being—your heart, your soul, until you *made* the words your own. Yes, *yes*!"

"*Actually*," Billie continued, "I made it with refrigerator magnets. You know, ones with words on them that you line up into sentences."

Patsy's admiration was unswerving. "Refrigerator magnets," she sighed. "You people from Massachusetts are so clever. Or are refrigerator magnets a lesbian thing?"

As they turned and walked back to the house, Patsy said, "I don't know how to explain this exactly. I'm a level-headed, self-sufficient 39-year old woman. And yet, being with you. . . ." Her voice trailed off.

"Let's sit on the steps for a minute." Patsy said. "What I'm trying to tell you is how crazy I feel—how once you stepped out of that forest green Ford Explorer a part of me that has lain dormant for all these years woke up. You're a hale and hardy wind sweeping the sedentary cobwebs from my life."

"Patsy," Billie said in what she hoped wasn't too parental a tone, "what's happening here is a classic case of transference and counter-transference. You are exalting me to undeserved heights. Not that I'm not flattered."

Patsy beamed. "All that terminology—Billie, you're so brilliant."

Frustrated, Billie thought, "Or it could just be your basic infatuation stage. I guess I can't be very objective."

So they sat watching the darkening sky, each lost in her own thoughts—which were, of course, about each other. After a while, Patsy slipped inside and brought out two tall glasses of lemonade.

She handed a glass to Billie, wondering why her body tingled when their fingers met. "Wait," she said and ran to the garden. She returned with two sprigs of mint, one for each glass. As the two women sipped their drinks, the crickets called and the lightning bugs put on a show. Prince lay in the grass, snoring lightly.

"It doesn't get any better than this," Billie said, and Patsy knew she was right.

Why did Billie have to return to the motel, Patsy thought. She could stay in Oak's room. It could be like a sleep over party! They could stay up late, have milk and cookies and maybe some of that Kahlua that Oak kept stashed under her bed.

But Patsy never voiced her idea. For some reason, asking Billie to stay the night crossed a line. It wasn't exactly the lesbian thing, because Patsy knew that Billie was too much of a lady to put the moves on her. No it was something else. Patsy turned to Billie, as if her face might hold the answer.

And in a way it did.

With moonlight illuminating her skin, Billie's features softened, her eyes seemed deep pools of wisdom and comfort. A rush of emotion swept through Patsy, but this wasn't the excitement she'd felt upon learning Billie was a lesbian, this wasn't the awe that had filled her when she learned Billie was a writer—no, it was instead a sense of falling, a gentle, safe falling in. . . .

Beep-beep. Billie's Casio Triple Sensor watch signaled ten o'clock. "I guess I'd best be off," she said, setting down her empty glass. She normally would have rinsed the glass in the sink so that Patsy wouldn't have to deal with sticky sugar residue in the morning, but she knew if she entered Patsy's kitchen there'd only be two ways she'd be leaving it—twenty minutes later with a heart full of pain or tomorrow morning with a heart full of pain. She didn't know which was worse, and she didn't want to find out.

So Billie stood up, smoothed her tan trousers over her canvas hiking boots, her starched white shirt a little less crisp. "I had a wonderful evening, Patsy, one I will remember for a long, long time." Billie paused, then added, "I hope things work out with you and Pete."

That was a lie, of course, but she couldn't very well say, "I hope you come out and have a emotionally fulfilling, sexually satisfying relationship with a fine upstanding lesbian."

Patsy looked so sad right then, that Billie knelt down and took her hands. "Keep reaching for the 'more'. If you can't have it with your family, at least have it for yourself."

Wordlessly, Patsy followed Billie to the Explorer, watched her swing her body gracefully into the driver's seat. Billie rolled down the window, her mind flashing on the "kiss in the rain" scene from *Desert Hearts*. If only it was pouring, then Patsy might lean through the open window and . . . but no, she'd have to step up onto the running board and kind of clench the door frame and besides wouldn't their roles be reversed? Billie shook the thought from her head.

"Good night," she called as she started the engine. "Good-bye," she whispered as she shifted into first gear.

By Moonlight

Slowly, Patsy walked back into her house. The kitchen seemed transformed, forever changed by the presence of Billie Bold. She wandered up to her bedroom and oddly enough felt the presence of Billie there too, although Billie had never gone up to the second story. Patsy undressed slowly, looked at herself in the mirror. Her body seemed transformed as well.

Patsy looked at her breasts. They seemed fuller, rounder than before. Pete, never onc to gracefully manage a compliment, had told her early in their marriage, "They'll do. They'll do."

Her arms and legs were tan and lightly muscled from the work around the farm. Cher's muscles were admired and praised; she'd even made all those health club commercials because of them. But Pete never complimented Patsy's muscle tone. She bet that, given the opportunity, Billie would.

Distractedly, Patsy wondered—when it came to bodies, did lesbians have a different value system than men? After all, on some level, when a woman looked at another woman's body, she was seeing her own. Did that make lesbians narcissistic? Or did it make heterosexual coupling inherently clumsy? Clumsy. That was a fitting word to describe her and Pete's love-making.

She wondered what Billie and her lovers were like in bed. No, not what they did physically, she wasn't so unimaginative that she couldn't envision how tongues, fingers, nipples and all the other parts worked between two women. But what words were spoken that brought them into bed? What did they say to each other during lovemaking, and most importantly, what happened afterwards? Did they smile into each others eyes? Did they feel that bonding she'd felt with Michael?

Billie put her clothes back on and walked downstairs. She pulled a white sheet of paper out of Pete's ink jet printer. She hesitated before putting pen to paper, then wrote quickly. She called to Prince and together they got into Patsy's Geo. Maintaining her courage and sense of direction, she quickly reached Bull Dyke Ranch, tacked the note to the gate, then headed home.

Passing Thoughts

Billie Bold drove past the mailbox of Pete, Patsy, Peace and Prince at eight the next morning. When she'd talked to Foxie and Mamie earlier, explaining the directions mishap, she'd omitted last night's activities.

Mamie had told Billie that B.J. and Charlie had stopped by the night before and had invited the three of them to dinner at their ranch—Diesel Dyke Acres—that evening. Grinning at her luck in catching all four women in one place, Billie had set off happily, allowing only a small pang of wistfulness as she passed the Plain's mailbox.

Between sips of instant cappuccino from her non-spillable Java Jitters mug, Billie nibbled on a low-fat granola bar. She glanced at the square, sturdy farmhouse and thought, "There, but for the grace of God, go I."

"But I can't live Patsy's life for her," Billie said, again wishing for a cat so she wouldn't be talking to herself so much.

"Still," she wondered, "how hard would it be for

Pete to leave his carrots behind for an evening and walk into the field with his wife?"

Sleeping in past 7:00 a.m. for the first time in years, Patsy did not hear as much as sense Billie's Explorer driving past. She'd gone to bed in nothing but a filmy teddy that she'd bought a year after Peace was born, in hopes of reviving what was left of her and Pete's romantic life. But on the night that she modeled it for her husband, all he'd said about the slinky blue negligee was that it was made out of a synthetic fabric with non-natural dyes and she'd be lucky if it didn't give her a rash.

So Patsy had tucked the nightie in a bottom drawer, where, as the years went by, it got buried under cotton long underwear and rag wool socks.

However, before climbing into bed last night, Patsy had dug it out and slipped it on. She'd gone to sleep with visions of Billie Bold floating through her head and then, apparently, down toward the lower regions of her body, regions that seemed to have awakened from a very long slumber.

Bull Dyke Ranch

Billie pulled to a stop outside the gates of Bull Dyke Ranch. With a yellow legal pad in one hand and her gold-plated pen in the other, she began making notes.

In the wind-swept, sun-soaked land of southwest Iowa, off a dusty back road, stands the gate to Bull Dyke Ranch, home to two women who once opened another set of gates—gates into the brave, new world of female homosexuality—for me. Today, I stand on that dirt road, thirty-four years after I entered "the life," and although my feet are not shod with loafers, they still feel light—

Billie broke off her writing, making a mental note to edit out the excessive verbosity, as she saw a sheet of paper fluttering in the breeze. "Billie," it read, and just as Billie untacked it from the wooden gate and was about to unfold it, a deep voice rang out.

"As I live and breathe, it's Billie Bold."

There stood Mamie, silver-haired and gorgeous.

She threw her arms out and gave Billie a big hug. "My and haven't the years been good to you!"

Mamie and Foxie's place was a rambling farmhouse. Mamie led Billie into the kitchen where Foxie was washing dishes.

"Billie," Foxie cried, giving her a soapy hug. "How long has it been?"

Basking in the glow of Foxie and Mamie's love, Billie suddenly remembered her tape recorder. "Do you mind if I record all this? For my article."

For the next three hours the three talked about old days and how they had ended up in Iowa.

"So when Mamie's father got sick, we both moved out here to take care of him. Mamie inherited the place after he died."

"What about the neighbors?" Billie asked.

"Folks accept us in their closed-mouth way—out of respect for Mamie's parents, I guess. Not to mention, we spend our money in town instead of WalMart."

After a lunch of fruit salad and tuna sandwiches (Billie tried not to think about dolphins), Billie gathered up her things.

"Glad you'll be joining us later at Charlie and B.J.'s," Foxie said. "We were thrilled when they decided to buy up the old McCartney Ranch. You'll be amazed what they've done with the place."

"Sounds terrific," Billie said. And then she was off to the motel room to journal her impressions.

Back in the Explorer, bouncing along the country road, Billie felt as if she were galloping on a million dollar mare, high in the saddle of life.

Refueling

As she drove by the farmhouse again, Billie wondered what Patsy was doing and had to resist the urge to stop in. Not that she really had the time.

"And not that anyone invited you, Ms. Billie," she chastised herself. Whatever she was to Patsy—a quickly forgotten stranger, her first quirky lesbian or simply a bright spot in an otherwise slow week—Billie was and would remain a passerby on Patsy's highway.

Besides, how many times had Billie sabotaged her dreams to answer a momentary tug on her heart? She was here to research Foxie, Mamie, B.J. and Charlie. She was here to capture the essence of a time gone by and the players in it, not to partake in a quick summer fling. She was here to shape a story that would—

Skreeeech!!! Billie slammed on the brakes and swerved to avoid a dog in the road. "Prince," she muttered, restarting the engine. The chocolate lab just wagged his tail and loped back toward the farmhouse.

Back in town, Billie stopped at a Gas Up! station to

get fuel for the Explorer, ice for the cooler and a package of Grandma's gingerbread cookies for herself. As she paid for her purchases, she noticed that the young woman behind the counter, whose name tag read "Sam," wore freedom rings around her neck. Billie wondered if she knew what they were. Double-checking to make sure no one else was around, she ventured, "I like your necklace."

"Thanks," Sam answered. "So, I take it you're the lesbian reporter writing about Diesel Dyke Acres."

Billie was caught off guard. "And just how did you come to that conclusion?" she asked.

"It's a small town. Fourteen eight-five, please."

Billie handed her a twenty.

"Anyway Jim at the Covered Bridges Motel is a friend of mine. We homos stick together."

"Do your parents know?"

"That you're doing research? No. Should they?"

"I meant do they know about you?"

"Why is that the first question everyone asks? Why not, do you have to take a lot of shit in school? Or do you have an escape plan? No, my mom does not know. Does yours?"

Billie leaned against the counter. "Well, to be honest, we don't much talk about it. Although she did figure it out years ago."

"My mom and I don't talk much either." Sam admitted. She tugged on her freedom rings. "I got these at Prairie Lights in Iowa City. My mom thinks they're 'happy' and 'colorful' and 'better than that black you wear all the time.'"

The bell on the door jangled and a man in jeans, boots and a Purina Horse Chow cap walked in. "Five-fifteen is your change, ma'am." Sam said, pushing the money towards Billie. "Have a good day."

Billie grinned. "Have a good life," she replied.

Back in her motel room, Billie turned up the air conditioner and sat down to go over her notes. As she typed on her PowerBook, she felt something rub in her back pocket. The note! She'd forgotten all about it. Billie unfolded it and read, "If you'd like to join me for another walk when the 'summer red sky screams out for the moon' drop by tonight. I'll be here."

Billie felt a warm rush and it wasn't the August heat, either. She reached for the phone, having had covertly viewed, then memorized, Patsy's number last night.

Patsy was chain-sawing dead branches when the phone rang. As fate would have it, she'd revved down the saw just in time to catch the last couple of rings. She picked up the cordless phone and walked towards the house for better reception.

"Hello?"

"Hi. This is Billie Bold." Patsy felt suddenly hot, and it wasn't just the sweat she'd built up in the yard.

"Got your note. I'd love to join you. But I'm interviewing my friends tonight. Is 9:30 or 10:00 all right?"

"Of course," Patsy said. "Finish your interviews. That's why you're here. Drop over when you're done."

"Is that why I'm here?" wondered Billie. Then she was hit by a flash of inspiration. "If you'd like to join me tonight and watch me work, I'd be pleased to have you.

I could come by and pick you up."

"Wow," Patsy mused to herself, "Up until yesterday I'd never a met a single lesbian and tonight I could meet a whole slew of them. But would driving with Billie draw too much attention. . . ? "

"Patsy? Are you there? " Billie asked.

"Yes, and I'd like to go, but I'll meet you there."

After a short nap and cool shower, Billie went downstairs to get her tarot cards out of Janeway. As she neared the manager's office, she overheard two people talking.

"First they inherit George's farm, then they buy up the McCartney place, now there's a les-bee-an in a big fancy. . . whatever they call them vehicles, anyway Madeline, they're gonna take over this town."

"Aw, Emmie, don't get your drawers in a knot. It's too damn hot."

Billie took this opportunity to walk past the office.

"That's her," she heard the first woman say. "I know it because they walk different than normal gals. Bigger steps. Think she heard us?"

"Nayh."

Back in her room, Billie thought about small town chatter. Maybe inviting Patsy to Diesel Dyke Acres was a mistake. Rumors would start, slander would run rampant, lives would be ruined. "I should call her." Billie thought. "Tell her it's okay to back out."

Then she laughed. "How classically codependent of me. Patsy is a grown-up. She can take care of herself."

So, Billie took the tarot cards out of their velvet drawstring bag and shuffled the round deck. Although she had time for only the simplest of readings, she took several breaths from her lower belly until she felt at one with—if not the universe—at least with the orange shag carpet beneath her feet.

Billie closed her eyes, posed a question in her head, then spoke it out loud. "Great Goddess Higher Spirit Power," she intoned, "provide me with guidance in the matter of Patsy Plain and my over-eager libido."

Then, with intention, she drew a single card from the deck. Secretly, she hoped it would be an inspiring card like the Shaman of Discs, which featured a powerful woman riding a sure-footed mule down her dharma path.

She flipped the card. The Wheel of Fortune. This card, with its images of birth, death, sex and magic always overwhelmed Billie. Its message, according to the book, was that her future was in the hands of the fates and she might as well surrender to the flow.

"The Wheel of Fortune" she muttered. "My life is a game show and my priestess is Vanna White."

Diesel Dyke Acres

Billie arrived at Charlie and B.J.'s early, in order to give them advance warning about Patsy. But Billie was immediately gathered in with hugs and backslaps and a hundred questions, so when Patsy's red Geo pulled up fifteen minutes later, Billie barely had time to explain.

"The more, the merrier," Charlie said, shaking Patsy's hand. Besides Mamie, Foxie, Charlie and B.J., there were two resident artists, Toni and Terri. Toni was a boisterous woman from North Dakota who created clay pieces "influenced by plant forms and magic-realism patterning." Terri was from L.A. and after recovering from urban deprivation had begun creating boldly colored, sprawling paintings of blue cows, purple porches and yellow tractors.

As Patsy chatted with the artists, Billie recalled that Patsy was suffering from conversation deprivation. Mildly jealous, she wondered if last night had meant nothing more than that.

Next Billie and Patsy were introduced to three

young women from the university—Mikki, Molly and Michele. "Our summer interns," B.J. announced with amused pride. "Part of the lesbian communal living project here at Diesel Dyke Acres."

"We're studying the historical ramifications of mid-seventies lesbian cooperative housing experiments," Michele explained.

"I didn't know I was an historical experiment," commented Billie, remembering her days in Tennessee.

"Are you related, by any chance, to Oak Plain?" Mikki asked Patsy.

"She's my daughter. Do you know her?"

"We go back to freshman year together—we were in the same dorm. As a matter of fact," Mikki laughed, "we were both in the same coming out—"

Michele elbowed her in the ribs. "Uh—we were both coming out of the dorm at the same time and nearly tripped... tripped over each other. That's how we met."

"That's a very amusing story," Patsy said, as Mikki, Michelle and Billie exchanged quick, furtive glances.

Then B.J. announced that supper was ready and everyone headed to the backyard, where the table was piled high with turkey dogs, tempeh burgers, corn on the cob, coleslaw, potato salad and a slew of condiments. The "family-sized" jar of mayonnaise nearly brought tears to Billie eyes, as she realized how long it had been since she'd felt like part of a family.

Fortunately, she was able to check her emotions and maintain her researcher's objectivity as she heaped a generous helping of marshmallow-rich ambrosia on her plate. "Cracker food," Charlie laughed as Billie downed a massive spoonful of the rich, sweet glop.

Charlie herself was spreading duck paté on a slice of focaccio bread. "Since when did you become a gourmet snob?" Billie laughed back.

"In my old age," Charlie answered. "My mother was always harping on me to eat better. Seems I had to wait until she died until I could take her advice."

"If your mother could see you today," B.J. said, wiping barbecue sauce off her face. "Remember when she finally found out about us? For her, the worst thing wasn't that we were lesbians, or that I was white, or even that I was Jewish, but that I was a 'Yankee from New Hampshire who couldn't cook worth a damn!'"

Then Billie asked, "What's with the names of these ranches? Bull Dyke Ranch. Diesel Dyke Acres. Sounds awfully blatant for middle America."

"We didn't start it," Foxie explained. "After B.J. and Charlie showed up, somebody caught on that lesbians were buying land here. We heard snickers, little asides—'Here come the gals from Bull Dyke Ranch.' So one day, Mamie made up two signs, *Diesel Dyke Acres* and *Bull Dyke Ranch*. Carved up those letters real nice. We hung 'em up and wouldn't you know, the nasty comments disappeared."

"Reclaiming language is a classic empowerment tool," commented Michele.

"So, overall, you all get along," Billie said. "Sort of like *Northern Exposure*."

"That would be stretching it," Charlie said.

"Stretching it a lot," said B.J.

On the Porch

After supper, Billie moved everyone to the porch. Revving up her PowerBook, she began her questions.

"Tell me about your sense of family in the mid-sixties. What was it like and how has it changed? How did you integrate butch and femme into your daily lives? What were the roles of the bars? How did the coming of the hippies and free love change your lives?"

"Billie," Foxie said, "you were bookish thirty years ago and you're bookish today. We were just living our lives. . ."

"But," B.J. chimed in, "she raises a good point—"

And the discussion was off. Patsy slid her wicker chair closer to Billie and her interviewees. She'd been spellbound the entire evening. To think that such vital and fascinating women had been living just twenty minutes down the road while she stayed at home, chain sawing fallen trees and baby-sitting her husband.

"Butch. Femme." Mamie was saying, "It's just a sexual energy that grew clothes."

"The problem is everyone went to extremes. We got stuck taking butch/femme too seriously—though we were no worse than the hets and their gender roles."

"You can't compare us with straights. A man's sexual prowess isn't tied up with pleasing his woman. But a butch's whole purpose is to please her femme."

"Back then, it *meant* something for a woman to wear pants. In this decade, butch and femme are just fashion statements."

As the debate swirled around her, Patsy's eyes turned to Billie fingers, which flew over the gray and white keyboard. So not only was Billie a writer, accountant and therapist, but she was a decent typist too. Again, Patsy was awed.

Awed? Patsy sat back for a minute. She was a sensible woman; what was going on here? Why was she so engrossed, overly-absorbed and unrealistically infatuated with Billie? She'd never acted this way before.

Again she turned to the tall, graying stranger from the East and watched Billie's fingers. For a sudden, shocking moment, Patsy wished *she* were the keyboard. "My, God," Patsy thought, the pieces falling into place, "Could I be in love with Billie Bold?"

Nearly immune to the conversation flying about—"Free love also meant being used by the tourists, straight gals who wanted to play but then go home to hubby and the bridge club"—Patsy realized that she didn't love Pete, had never loved Pete, had never loved anyone, not in the physical, passionate sense. "Does this mean I'm a lesbian? Bisexual? Or just a tourist?"

Patsy looked up at all the faces on the porch. In the

soft glow of the setting sun, they became the most honest, self-affirming sight she had ever seen. Sisterhood. Acceptance. Family.

"How can you believe such drivel, Foxie? There were divisions then just as now. The racism, the classism, the insults—"

"I'm not denying that. What I'm saying is that there was a belief, as brief and misinformed as it was, that women could change the world, that lesbians could overcome the social dysfunction and transform—"

Billie's fingers stopped. "Battery's used up," she announced. "Perhaps this would be a good time to take a break."

Everyone stood and stretched. "How 'bout some coffee. Cold drinks?" B.J. offered. As the group shuffled off to the kitchen, Billie turned and found herself face to face with Patsy.

"Billie, I have to talk to you. I think I've just discovered something wonderful."

"Yes, tonight has been full of revelations, but I need to jot down a few thoughts before I lose them."

"But—"

"Please, just a minute."

And as Billie wrote in her intense yet not frantic manner, Patsy was again captivated by Billie's fingers—how she gripped her pencil, neither too hard nor too lightly, how the graphite, for the slightest of seconds, was neither on the pencil nor on the paper, but somewhere in between. Wasn't her life now like that, she thought, knowing instinctively in her very being that she, like the graphite was about to jump off and fly out into new, uncharted space.

"Billie, do you still want to come over tonight?"

"Of course. You don't think I'd forgotten, do you?" Although, as a matter of fact, Billie had not only forgotten about tonight, but about Patsy's presence altogether, so engrossed was she in the surge of woman-energy that had filled the room. What did she, Billie Bold, need with fantasies of unavailable straight women, anyway?

Then she looked into Patsy's eyes, gazed at the curve of her jawline and the curve of her breast, and remembered that sometimes fantasies turn into reality. . . .

Voices floated in from the kitchen and the crowd began coming towards them. Patsy and Billie stepped back from one another, their hearts and bodies re-kindled once more.

The talk turned to memories and stories of the old days. Around nine, Foxie got up and stretched. "If the four of us are still going on that fishing trip tomorrow, then I, for one, need to get some sleep. Do you still want to do more interviewing on Saturday, Billie?"

Billie did and they reaffirmed plans. As the younger women cleaned up the kitchen, Patsy and Billie headed out the door.

"I know this sounds funny, after that big supper, but I'm in the mood for a late night snack," said Patsy as they headed toward their cars. Okay if I whip something up when we get back?"

"Sure. I'd like to stop by the motel and wash up anyway. I can meet you in half an hour." Billie said.

"I *have* running water," Patsy teased, wondering if being with all those lesbians had caused some flirtatious energy to rub off on her.

So Billie agreed to skip the motel and while Patsy started the Geo, Billie started the Explorer and under the bright moon on that warm August night the forest green sport utility vehicle followed the cherry red sub-compact back to the farmhouse on Rural Route 9. Each driver was lost in her own thoughts of doubt and desire, concern and confusion, lust and, well, lust.

Revelation

"Gosh, I'm hot," Billie said, as she stepped into Patsy's kitchen. " I mean, I'm warm. Overheated."

"Relax," Patsy said. "I'm hot too."

"What does she mean?" Billie wondered, setting down the six-pack of beer she'd brought in.

"So, do you want to take a shower?" Patsy asked.

"Together?" thought Billie.

"The upstairs bathroom is more pleasant. We added the downstairs one when Oak was ten, figuring she'd spend hours in front of the mirror, fixing her hair or playing with make-up. But she never went through that phase."

Patsy led Billie up the stairs, stopping at the linen closet to pull out a fluffy mauve towel and matching washcloth. "Holler if you need anything. I'll be downstairs."

Puttering in the kitchen, Patsy marveled at how easily she shifted between roles, acting as casually as if Billie were an out-of-state cousin she was putting up for the night. Then, as she heard the shower come on, it dawned on her that Billie was naked up there, the water streaming down her hair, riveting through her shoulder blades to the small of her back. Or between her well shaped, unfettered breasts.

Patsy looked down, realized she'd been standing motionless for several moments with an artichoke in one hand, a knife in the other and an unfamiliar but not unwelcome ache between her legs.

There in that moment, with gourmet vegetable in hand, Patsy Plain put it all together—the sexuality chapters in *Our Bodies, Ourselves* , the giggly confessions of her women friends, the sex experts on Sally Jesse Raphael. In all her adult years, she'd never felt anything close to the passion they described. Patsy had concluded that she was simply defective. But that wasn't it at all, she knew now.

"I'm not abnormal," Patsy cried out. "I'm a lesbian!"

Just then, the shower water cut off and the phone rang, which momentarily confused Patsy, as if one were connected to the other.

If she had thought about it she would have let the machine pick up. But still in her half-dazed moment of revelation, she held the receiver to her mouth. "Hello?"

It was Pete. "Just got back from a highly stimulating debate, 'The Size of Our Carrots: When Is Big Too Big?' Gosh Pats, there are men from all over the heartland here, sharing our stories about root vegetables. It's almost as good as being on-line."

"That's really exciting, Pete," she said. "I've had a breakthrough too." Then she caught herself, realizing this might not be the best time to share her recent discovery.

"Uh, huh," Pete said. "And what's that?"

"I, uh, it's just that.. I finally got out the chainsaw and cut those dead branches off the cottonwood."

"Well, I'm real happy for you, hon, but I gotta go. Be back on Friday, in time for a late dinner."

She hung up the phone, cut an "x" in the artichoke and put it in a pot of boiling water, aware that this was her very first act as a newly confirmed lesbian. (Unless you counted answering the phone call from her husband, which she didn't.)

She gathered up some faded, fruit-shaped candles that Pete's parents had sent and put them in the middle of the table. Patsy thought they were hideous and was pleased to have the opportunity to burn them.

Earlier, she'd brought down Oak's portable CD player. Although Patsy hadn't bonded to music like most adolescents, she knew it was an important part of creating atmosphere. She inserted the *Enya* CD her daughter had given her for Christmas.

As Patsy checked on the artichoke, she heard footsteps on the stairway and turned. At the door to the kitchen stood Billie. She was even more stunning than the day Patsy had first laid eyes on her, which was only yesterday, come to think of it.

Billie wore a natural-weave, button-down shirt (made from pesticide-free cotton, Patsy was sure), soft black jeans and thick sandals, that despite their inherent clunkiness, somehow looked elegant on her. Her wavy salt and pepper hair was still damp and her skin glowed with a radiance that must have come naturally with being gay.

Patsy had planned to blurt out her homosexual revelation right away, but now, looking at the resplendent woman standing in her kitchen, she was practically speechless. "I'm going to . . . take a bath," she told Billie. "Except that our snack is still cooking, and. . . ."

"Don't worry," Billie assured her, "I'll take care of everything. Would you like a beer with your bath?" Billie pulled a Phyllis Wheatly wheat ale out of the refrigerator and this time twisted off the cap.

As Patsy soaked in the tub (her first bath as a lesbian) she felt wonderfully free. Everything about her marriage now made sense—the lack of romance, the lack of sex drive, the lack of interest. She wasn't a failed wife; she was a normal lesbian.

Billie would understand. Billie, wondrous Billie, whose unclothed body had occupied this very space only minutes ago. How lucky she was to have Billie step into her life.

Patsy toweled off and slipped into a pair of high-cut underwear and a sports bra. Over these, she pulled on a pair of soft white trousers and a deep red tank top that Pete considered trashy.

The house was warm and she really didn't need any more clothes. Still, she delved into Oak's closet, and came up with a gray University of Iowa Women's Basketball sweatshirt with a ripped-off collar and cut-off sleeves. Feeling dubious, she pulled it over her head. "It's my first night as a lesbian," she decided, "I guess it's okay if I don't know what to wear." With fresh white running shoes on her feet, she descended the steps.

Her kitchen had been transformed; the lights were dim, *Enya* was playing and Billie Bold was there, placing the perfectly steamed artichoke on the table. Billie looked up, saw Patsy in that ripped sweatshirt and emitted a low appreciative whistle. "East Coast Blazer Dyke Falls for Rough and Tumble Rural Gal," ran the headline in her head.

At that moment, Billie Bold, the last lesbian cliché, the dyke who'd seen it all, tried it all, and still felt nothing, knew she'd come home. There, in a simple Iowa kitchen she fell hopelessly in love with Patsy Plain, a self-sufficient, married straight woman, who until yesterday had never met a lesbian.

"Patsy, you are gorgeous," Billie said, stammering slightly. "You're so 'in your body,' radiating such quiet animal magnetism and dignified self-worth."

"Funny," Patsy said softly, "I was about to say the same thing about you."

Heart to Heart

"Shall I light the candles?" Billie asked, pulling out a chair for Patsy. Patsy nodded a simple "yes."

As she lit the kiwi, pineapple, then tangerine-shaped candles, Billie smiled into the glowing light. Patsy drew up her courage, knowing it was now or never.

"Billie," she said, "something big happened tonight."

"I know," Billie said, sipping her beer.

"I don't just mean meeting all those women or hearing their stories. I mean about me. Being there, seeing all of them, then frankly, thinking about you showering upstairs—well, it came to me. I'm. . . I'm a lesbian, Billie. I've been one my whole life and it took you to show me the way."

"I know." Billie repeated, more softly this time.

"How?" Patsy was stunned. "How could *you* have known?"

"When you walked into the kitchen, I saw that your aura had changed. Your whole body is giving off a luminous lesbian energy."

"Wow." Patsy said, amazed.

"So now that you know that I know that you know, let's have a toast to your new-found knowledge." Billie lifted her beer. "To you, Patsy."

"Oh, I don't know," Patsy said, clinking her mug. "Patsy doesn't sound very lesbian. Maybe I should try my initials, like B.J. Some combination from my full name—Patricia Remington Oakshire Plain."

"P.P.?" asked Billie.

"Sounds like toddler bathroom talk."

"P.R.?"

"A publicity firm."

"P.O.?" Billie offered.

"Might as well be 'U.S. Mail.'"

"Actually, among many lesbians, Patsy Cline is highly venerated. Patsy is a fine, upstanding lesbian name."

"Really?" Patsy sighed happily. "Patsy it is, then."

As glad as Billie was to facilitate Patsy's coming out and embracing of her given name, the question of this farm wife's attraction towards her was still up in the air. It wouldn't be right to rush things, and yet. . . .

"I'd hate to see the artichoke get cold," Billie said. "Shall we dig in?"

"Of course."

"Just why did you choose an artichoke, anyway?"

"Oh, I just have a thing for the 'A' vegetables. Artichokes, avocados, asparagus. Pete thinks they're snooty vegetables, but I like to think that they've just got a good publicity agent."

Then they laughed in the candlelit room, sharing the small joke with an intimacy of souls who have spent many lifetimes together.

"And I'd thought you'd chosen an artichoke because it's such a lesbian vegetable."

"And how is that?" Patsy asked, intrigued.

"Let me demonstrate." Billie pulled off a leaf, placed it in her mouth, then, closing teeth upon it, slowly pulled it out in a motion reminiscent of a very skilled, very sensuous strip tease.

"Oh, my," Patsy murmured. "Do that again."

Billie did, and then Patsy did, undressing the artichoke in a slow dance of tongues, teeth and discreet gulping motions.

"And now only the heart remains," said Billie.

Patsy said nothing and Billie noticed tears in her eyes. "What's wrong?" she asked in a deeply compassionate way.

"It's, it's just that I want to give you more. You deserve more than this old kitchen and dusty, fruit-shaped candles."

"No!" Billie insisted. "Don't you understand? I've had it all—Key West, the Russian River, The Dinah Shore Golf Tournament. I've hot tubbed at the Ruby Slipper in Taos, been pampered at Gabriel's in P-Town, but that's not what I want, not—" she paused, "what I need. What I need is a strong-hearted, clear-eyed woman from the heartland of America."

Shocked at her raw confession, Billie sat back in her chair, the voice of her inner child shouting in her head. "Now you've done it. You've blurted out your needs, wants and desires and set me up for another broken heart. More pain. More abandonment issues. Leave. Get up now and go. Join Foxie and the rest on their fishing trip. Bond in their sisterly love. Or drive back to Michigan. Find some hot biker woman and play out your desires in an Elizabethan fantasy. Live out your life in your head or your genitals, but don't get your heart involved, because—"

"Enough!" cried Billie.

"Billie?" asked Patsy, "what's going on?"

"Sorry, my inner child was throwing a temper tantrum."

Patsy looked puzzled.

"I'm scared, that's all."

"Scared that this is outrunning you? Scared that you and I are already bonded together, 'solidly, intimately and inextricably'?"

"Why yes. How did you know?" Billie asked.

"That's the way they described it in this silly book that Pete gave me for Christmas. Imagine, Pete thinking that buying me a romance novel could make up for twenty years of detached indifference."

Billie looked deep into Patsy's eyes and said softly, "But I can."

"Yes, you can."

And Patsy took the artichoke and, with the skill of a caring surgeon, removed the heart from its thorny center. "I give you my heart, Billie Bold."

Billie accepted it, breaking off a small piece. "And I give my heart to you," she said, passing it back to Patsy, who tenderly chewed the rest.

Dancing the "I'm One Too" Step

Enya had long ago spun out. Billie pushed back her chair. "Just a minute," she said, fiddling with the player. The unmistakable voice of Patsy Cline sang out, "I fall to pieces. . . ."

"Care to dance?" Billie asked.

Shyly, Patsy rose from her chair and walked across the tired linoleum of the kitchen floor. She'd danced with her girlfriends in high school, getting ready for Legion Hall dances, but this felt quite different. Once she let herself relax, however, slow dancing in the arms of Billie Bold felt completely natural. She buried her face in Billie's neck.

"What kind of creature are you," Patsy whispered in her ear, "roaming the country like the wind, no, like a hurricane, no, more like a northwesterly storm front, tearing away false fronts and exposing tender truths?"

"I hope that was a rhetorical question," Billie answered, as they continued to move together, their bodies in perfect harmony. Patsy sighed, feeling the crush of Billie's breasts against her own, an unfamiliar but breathtaking sensation, and not only because Billie was holding her too tight.

"Sorry," Billie said, "I always want to hold close those I cherish, but sometimes I take it a little too literally."

Patsy Cline continued to sing and they continued to dance, small steps, close steps. When Billie's thigh brushed between her legs, Patsy felt a rush of pleasure. She shuddered in quiet ecstasy.

The next song was peppier, and as Billie spun and dipped Patsy, they both broke into giggles at their playfulness. "Are all lesbians as wonderful as you, Billie?" she asked as the song ended.

"No one is as wonderful as I am," laughed Billie, "except you."

Your Cheatin' Heart followed. Billie hoped that Patsy wouldn't get thrown off by the lyrics, but Patsy, who was off on a cloud of bliss, only looked up dreamily at Billie and said, "I didn't know that Oak had a Patsy Cline CD."

"It's mine," Billie said. "I brought it in from Janeway. Thought I'd surprise you."

"And what other surprises do you have for me?"

"Oh, I think it's your turn to show me a surprise," Billie whispered.

"I think you're right," Patsy whispered back.

And she led Billie Bold up the stairs.

Robust Rapture and Potent Pleasures

"Oh, yes! Yes! Yessss!" Patsy screamed in full bodied delight.

"Patsy, Patsy," Billie soothed, "I'm glad you like how I look with my shirt unbuttoned but perhaps you should pace yourself."

Patsy stretched across the formerly uneventful bed she had shared with Pete for over twenty years. Now, with candles lit and her husband's things stuffed in the closet, the bedroom felt cleansed. In fact, it had taken on a whole new essence—a place where human cravings belonged, where womanly ecstasy could thrive.

Pulling off Patsy's sweatshirt, Billie purred in deep arousal as she took in the curves of Patsy's tank-topped torso. Patsy smiled, aware of the feelings she was stirring in Billie. Then she could wait no longer. She leaned over and kissed Billie on the mouth. Overwhelmed by the unanticipated pleasure of the kiss, Patsy sank into the freshly laundered sheets.

But Billie held onto her and soon tongues and teeth, nipples and lips were engaged in a passion play of tasting and teasing. Billie had never experienced anyone like Patsy before: so fresh and innocent to Sapphic joys, yet so self-assured and willing to partake in lesbian ways.

As they continued to cavort, with a motion both swift and agile, Patsy flipped Billie over. As surprised as she was to find herself on her back, Billie was still more shocked to discover she liked it. Body on top of body, they moved now, in a horizontal dance of fierce pleasure. Thighs pressing, breasts firming, and that ache, that wonderful ache, spreading throughout.

Soon they could not stand the barrier of clothing and in a fine percussion symphony, zippers were unzipped, snaps unsnapped and Velcro ripped, followed by an unfastening of buttons, both brass and plastic, until not only their clothes, but the very outer trappings of their souls lay in a heap at the foot of the bed.

"Wait, wait," Patsy cried and for one terrible moment Billie was afraid that they'd gone too fast and Patsy would curl up in a tight ball of heterosexual denial or worse yet, monogamous guilt.

"Birth control." Patsy gasped. "We need birth control."

Billie laughed. "It doesn't work that way."

Patsy blushed. "Oh, right. Would you believe, Pete still uses rubbers. As back-up. Even though he's had a vasectomy. Even though we only have sex twice a year. And it's nothing like this."

"I can imagine," Billie said. "Although, frankly, I'd rather not."

Patsy laughed and pounced on top of her with a playful growl. They tickled and wrestled, then shifted into a more fervent motion.

"I feel powerful with you, Billie Bold," Patsy said, her voice low and seething with sex. "We are nature—primal, moving by instinct. We're like two lions, fierce and mighty."

"Lions, huh?" Billie said, "Gives a new twist the phrase 'lesbian pride.' Or should I say 'I am woman. Hear me roar?'"

Patsy groaned. "You're bad, Billie. Billie Bold is Billie Bad."

"No, I'm good. Billie Bold is very good."

And to prove her point, Billie moistened her index finger in Patsy's mouth and slid it down Patsy's body—between her breasts, over her stomach, and finally between her legs. As she moved her cupped hand over Patsy's hard bud of pleasure, they both drew in sharp ragged breaths, their hearts beating with lust and desire.

"Oh," Patsy rasped. "Oh." Her body was a quaking valley ready to split, a tidal wave rolling towards shore, a potent geyser ready to explode. Billie, caught in the powerful tempest of Patsy's desire, grew ripe, raw and ready.

"Now," Billie screamed to the goddess, the universe and several unnamed asteroid belts. "Oh, yes—now!" And as one, they came in an immensely powerful, deeply spiritual and perfectly synchronized simultaneous orgasm.

"Wow," Patsy said, a few minutes later, as their entwined bodies, minds and spirits slowly floated apart,

"Is lesbian love-making always like that?"

"Usually, it's not so understated," Billie said sleepily. "But let's cut ourselves some slack. After all, this is our first time together."

Pulling Billie close and then the sheet over both of them, Patsy yawned and fell into a blissful slumber.

Precious Hours

For the next few days, Patsy gave up chain sawing, welding, small engine repair and other farmwifely duties. Billie gave up writing, which was less traumatic seeing as she'd only been a writer for two days. They spent all their time together, making love, going on walks, talking about their lives.

They made love on the creek bank at dawn, on the porch swing at dusk, in the bathtub at night. Afterwards, they talked of their lives—memories of childhood, joys and sorrows, dreams still lingering. Twice they shared fantasies, enacted them and then discussed what worked and what didn't.

"We're . . . we're *processing*!" Patsy exclaimed, proud to be so quickly partaking in such a time-honored lesbian ritual. "Billie?"

"Yes?" Billie asked dreamily.

"Are all lesbians such noble creatures?"

Billie opened her eyes and spoke to the ceiling. "Perhaps we were, long ago, but now the modern world is stripping our nobility from us—along with our civil rights. Time was, before we were the subject of sociology courses and got the best lines on *Roseanne*, we were a simple, yet dignified people. Call it a ghetto, call it marginalized, but we stuck together and treated each other with respect." She paused, "Of course, I might be over-romanticizing. What do you think?"

Patsy considered briefly, then said, "I think the exploration of ghettoization versus assimilation of lesbian culture warrants examination, but considering the variety of subcultures within the greater community, how can one establish a base paradigm without deconstructing the historical aspects, which by doing so, destroys the very concept of the presupposition you set out to prove?"

"Patsy!" Billie exclaimed, "Where did you learn to talk like that?"

Patsy blinked, as if coming out of a trance. "I—I don't know. Maybe my dormant homosexual genes just clicked into place—"

"—activating your collective lesbian consciousness," concluded Billie. "Of course. Still, I haven't heard that kind of language since I was with my eighth lover, the sociology professor."

"Billie," Patsy said sadly, "My life with Pete seems so dull compared to yours."

"'The mass of men lead lives of quiet desperation,'" Billie quoted.

"Let me guess," Patsy teased. "You made that from refrigerator magnets. No wait, it's a political button. No—Melissa Etheridge."

"Uh, uh." Billie smiled.

"Chastity Bono? Sandra Bernhard? Candance Gingrich?"

"Nope, nope, and nope. Henry David Thoreau," Billie said.

"And he was gay too, right? "Patsy said.

"Not that I know of."

"Well," Patsy said, "you gays *are* always claiming the most interesting people for yourselves." She paused. "Oops. I guess I should say 'ourselves'."

"I guess," Billie said, her eyes gleaming, "we've just claimed another."

And they both dived into the sheets for another hour of ardent amour and luscious lovemaking.

On Thursday, they raided the pantry for Saran Wrap as they explored techniques heretofore unexperienced by Patsy.

A cold front had moved in, and while the drizzle dominated the out-of-doors, the bedroom was a cozy nest of rumpled sheets, burning candles and massage oil.

As they recovered from their fifth mutual orgasm of the morning, Billie propped herself up on her elbow. "Can I ask you something?" she ventured.

Patsy dreaded the question that she knew must come, the one they'd both been avoiding: the question of "What next?" and the rest of their lives. She braced herself.

"Are you getting enough penetration?" Billie asked.

"Oh—" Patsy said, surprised. "Is that all?"

Billie shrugged. "Well, I'm glad it's no big deal to

you. As a dyke, I'm a little sensitive about it."

Patsy kissed her on the forehead. "I didn't mean to hurt your feelings." She lay back in the sweet smelling sheets. "Penetration. Did you have something in mind?"

To tell the truth, Billie *had* been thinking about the vibrating dolphin/pearldiver dildo back in the Explorer, but somehow that didn't fit the mood. "Well, many women enjoy the sensation of penetration along with simultaneous stimulation of the nipples and/or clitoris," she explained.

"Billie, you sound like a sex manual," Patsy laughed.

"What I'm saying is—a girl only has so many hands. Surely you've heard jokes about women and cucumbers."

Patsy grinned and kissed Billie again, this time on the mouth. "I think I'm catching your drift. Wait just a minute." And she bounded downstairs to the kitchen. A few minutes later Patsy returned with a handful of freshly washed carrots. They both fell into a long bout of giggles.

An hour later, after three more deeply satisfying orgasms, Patsy turned to Billie and said, "After twenty years, I've finally come to appreciate that damned vegetable."

Bittersweet

Late Thursday afternoon, as a mild thunderstorm rolled through, Billie and Patsy could no longer avoid The Talk.

"What do you want to do?" Billie asked.

"Play with that avocado some more?" Patsy suggested.

"You know that's not what I meant."

Patsy looked down at the sheets. "I don't know."

"Pack your things and come with me. We'll go camping on the isle of Lesbos, go to the Gay Games in Amsterdam. We'll lose ourselves in laughter at Josie's Juice Joint or explore our inner babes at the Clit Club. I'll take care of you as we live off the steady wages I'll earn as a lesbian journalist."

"Whoa, Billie. Slow down."

But Billie was on a roll. "Or if life on the road doesn't suit you, we can buy a house together. I'll start up my practice again. We can live anywhere. Oak can visit on school breaks." She paused, "If it helps, I'll go with you when you break the news to Pete. I'll explain the historical, Puritan roots of America's sexual rigidity and how it breeds hatred of our own bodies, spiritual repression and homophobia."

Patsy shook her head slowly. "Pete will never understand. To him lesbianism is nothing more than two female models getting it on in Penthouse magazine. Or," she added bitterly, "in a graphic image file he's downloaded on his computer. He'd never be able to understand the magic or the passion, let alone the politics, of womanly love."

"Well then, he doesn't have to understand it. Or accept it. After all, it's your life."

"I don't know. Everything is happening too fast."

Billie leaned back against the pillows. "Yes, I suppose we could be madly projecting our unmet childhood needs on each other."

"No, it's more than that. Billie, you are on a great spiritual quest. You are a writer, a chronicler of your people, of *our* people. Last night, when we made love you said, 'I am the song, I am the storm, I am the singer in the storm.' You *are* the singer, Billie, and I don't want to silence your song."

"Oh, Patsy, I was only paraphrasing Holly Near."

Patsy raised an eyebrow, but continued. "Nonetheless, in this age when lesbians are conforming to societal roles and becoming attorneys, performance artists and co-parents, I don't want to be the one to dilute your raw power, your sacred journey. You are adventure and yellow legal pads and a sport utility vehicle named Janeway. You may be that Jill-of-all-trades, that last lesbian cliché, and if you are I will not keep you from your destiny."

Billie started to frame a retort, but Patsy stopped her. "Before you launch into a tirade about codependency, let me say that this is not only about you. I have responsibilities here. Yes, my life is dull. Excruciatingly boring. Deadening and depressing too. Pete is dim and uninteresting, but at least he is distant and remote. Oak, the one person I truly cherish, is away at school. My life lacks excitement, romance, intelligent conversation and now, it will lack you.

"And yet—yet there's this infernal sense of responsibility I have. To Pete, to Oak."

"What about to yourself?" Billie asked.

As if Billie hadn't spoken at all, Patsy went on. "Don't I owe something to them? What will it be like for them to live with the nasty whispers—'Pete Plain's old lady turned out to be a dyke and ran off with some lesbo journalist.' It would wreck their lives forever."

Billie doubted that last statement. People had a remarkable ability for recovery, she knew, but she didn't want to debate the matter. "I feel caught," she admitted to Patsy. "As a feminist, I want to acknowledge your truth and honor your decisions, and yet, as a sister, how can I abandon you to societally-induced self-hatred and internalized homophobia, not to mention a rotten sex life?"

Patsy smiled, a profoundly sad and sorrowful smile, a smile that seemed to stand for the deserted dreams of millions of women, who'd given themselves up for the good of their families.

Billie knew she could not change Patsy, knew she shouldn't even want to change her. So instead, she held her close and whispered. "Even though we've only known each other for a little more than 96 hours, even though we have absolutely no real world experience with each other and even though we're both totally immersed in the highly irrational infatuation stage of this fledging relationship, I know in my heart that no matter how long I live or how many lifetimes I live, you will be the only woman I'll ever be able to love with my whole being, my whole soul and my whole heart."

"Wow, " Patsy said.

That night they made love again, a slow, spiritual lovemaking during which their astral bodies ascended and joined as one, to part only when each contained the essence of the other deep within itself.

They held each other all night long—except when Billie had to get up to pee and Patsy had to go downstairs to let Prince, whom'd they completely forgotten about for the last two days, inside.

The Cold Cruel Dawn

As the first streaks of morning illuminated the sky Patsy could no longer fight off sleep. When she awoke four hours later, Billie was already downstairs, drinking a cup of coffee. Although she was freshly showered, her trousers had lost their crease and her starched shirt looked a bit crumpled. "Like my heart," thought Patsy.

Patsy walked up behind her, massaged her shoulders, then ran her hands through Billie's hair. Billie reached back and pulled Patsy into her lap, where she sat, first holding back the tears, then giving into them as Prince gnawed and slurped at his paw pads.

Billie shifted and Patsy stood up. Draining her coffee, Billie said, "I guess I'll be on my way."

Patsy sniffed and reached for a paper towel on which to blow her nose. Graciously, Billie pulled out a deep green bandanna, a bandanna the color of her eyes, the color of Janeway, why even, the color of the shirt Patsy was wearing the day they met. She handed it to Patsy who honked gratefully.

"Keep it," Billie said, "and not just because you've blown your nose in it. Keep it and remember me."

"Oh, Billie. I would say I'll never wash this bandanna, but. . . ."

So they laughed again until the laughter turned back into tears and Billie said, "If you want to write to me, you have my P.O. Box in Northampton. And my voice mail number. And the number of my cell phone."

"And your beeper." Patsy added.

"And my fax." Billie put in.

"And your e-mail address." Patsy said.

"Yes, that too." Billie paused. "In a world of instant connections, you'd think it would be impossible to feel such isolation," she smiled sadly, "but I do."

Straightening her shoulders, Billie took a deep breath and said, "I'll be in town for the next few days. More interviews and research. You can reach me at the motel. If you change your mind, just let me know and I'll be here.

Grabbing the green and purple gym bag, Billie walked out to the Explorer and tossed it in carelessly atop the otherwise meticulously packed items. She was very upset, Patsy realized.

The morning was clear and bright; it smelled of fresh rain and fresh starts. Patsy's heart screamed out, "Don't leave! Let me go with you!" But she couldn't say the words, could only watch as Billie opened the door, put one foot on the running board and—

"It's not supposed to end this way!" Billie cried, her voice full of anguish. "This is a *lesbian* romance. It's supposed to have a happy ending." They hugged each other tightly, their hearts pressed close.

"I will always remember you, Billie Bold."

"And I you, Patsy."

With tears streaming down her cheeks, Billie swung into the driver's seat. Janeway started up flawlessly. Billie rolled down the tinted window and looked out without a word. She drove to the end of the drive and shifted the Explorer into neutral, opened the door and leaned out. Her writer's mind took it all in: the farmhouse, the meadow, the porch swing, the chocolate lab named Prince, but mostly nature's wondrous creation, Patsy—Patsy Oakshire Plain of Madison County, Iowa. And just in case her brain slipped up, she reached for her leather-covered notepad to jot down her thoughts.

Driving Rain

Pete and Oak arrived that evening. Pete was full of tales of new carrot hybrids and guaranteed techniques for boosting root vegetable production. Oak was sulky, going up to her room immediately after Patsy's dinner of grilled fish, potatoes and canned peas. Pete had brought home a sixth place carrot cake from the convention's carrot bake-off, but Patsy couldn't eat any—she couldn't even *look* at a carrot without thinking of Billie.

Patsy went up to Oak's room and softly knocked on the door.

"Come in," Oak said grudgingly.

Patsy sat on the edge of her bed. "How was your week?" she asked. "Did you have fun with Chris?"

"It was okay."

"What did the two of you do?"

"Not much."

"Not much?" Patsy said, tousling her beloved daughter's hair. "Five days together and you only did 'not much'?"

"What did *you* do all week, Mom?" Oak asked.

Patsy balked. "Oh, not much."

Now this was interesting. "Mom, you had a whole week." Oak insisted, enjoying herself, "You must have done *something*."

"Some things are private, dear," Patsy said, standing up to leave the room. She paused. "Sweetheart, I hope you appreciate the sacrifices I've made for you."

"Uh, sure Mom." Oak answered, as Patsy closed the door.

Pete was catching up on his e-mail as Patsy passed his little office on her way outside. She sat on the porch swing, watching the last wisps of light disappear into the night.

Pete came out at ten. "Just finished chatting with some guy in Kentucky about the crumbling sense of community in this country. I sure do like that Internet. You okay? You've been kinda quiet all night."

"I'm fine, Pete."

"Well, I'm beat. You coming to bed?"

Although she had changed the sheets, stowed the candles and massage oil, and restored all of Pete's things to his side of the bed, Patsy couldn't get the feeling of Billie out of the bedroom. And with Pete so excited from the conference, he probably had sex on his mind. He'd probably want to play "Peter Rabbit and Farmer McGregor in the Lettuce Patch." Her stomach turned at the thought.

"Not yet. I just want to sit here a little longer."

Patsy stayed away from town for the next three days,

knowing Billie was at the Covered Bridges Motel. She knew if she saw Billie again, she wouldn't be able to resist going to her.

Tuesday was wet and cool; Patsy thought it a good time to resurface the countertop cutting board. However, the groceries were running low and Pete wanted to pick up the gourmet goose manure he'd special-ordered from Santa Cruz, so they took the truck into town. After loading two dozen bags of duck droppings onto the truck bed, Pete dropped Patsy off at the Safeway and headed to the Streep Street Cafe to chat with his pals.

Forty minutes later, they met outside the market, put the grocery bags into the cab and took off. As they neared the Gas Up!, Patsy saw the forest green Explorer pulling out of the station. And as it bumped onto the road just ahead of them, Patsy's whole world seemed to shift into misty slow motion. . . .

Three Way at the Four Way

Patsy could have sworn that the fog had entered the cab. Pete seemed faded and far, far away. Ahead was the Explorer, a single, misty car's length in front of them. Slowly, ever so slowly, both vehicles moved through a gray, hazy soup until they reached a four-way stop—heavily trafficked and awash in the thick drizzle. They seemed to wait there for hours.

Pete stared ahead at Janeway. In a disembodied voice, he commented, "That's an awfully fancy truck."

"It's not a truck," Patsy heard herself mumble, "It's a sport utility vehicle."

Pete looked at her and shrugged. "Whatever. Huh, look at the Massachusetts plates," she heard him say in that eerie, detached voice. "Must be that queer reporter that folks were talking about—the one with the funny haircut."

The Explorer's driver's side window slowly lowered and Billie's head appeared briefly, searching for a clear view before turning north. The Explorer turned left, onto the two lane highway, and Patsy caught a final glimpse of Billie as she drove off through the mist. . . .

"Billie!" Patsy screamed, "Billie!"

Patsy sat bolt upright in her bed. She gasped for air.

Comforting arms reached around her. "Another nightmare, honey?"

"Yes, the same one." Patsy said. "The four-way stop. Remember it?"

"Of course I do. I was there."

"I dreamed that—"

Billie reached out and pulled Patsy close. "You dreamed that I drove on, into the fog. But it's been six years now and that's not what happened, sweetheart."

"No." Patsy continued, half-asleep. "No, when Pete said, 'must be that queer reporter with the funny haircut,' I said, 'Yeah, and great breasts too.' He was so shocked that I was halfway out the door before he even noticed."

"And then you sprinted up to Janeway and with one strong, graceful movement—"

Patsy smiled, "I remember. . . ."

The Road Before Us

Patsy, hair dripping, grabbed the handle of the passenger door and pulled.

It was locked.

However, Billie—ever alert—immediately pressed a short series of buttons on the Explorer's master control panel. Patsy opened the door and jumped in, just as Billie was shifting into first gear.

"Sorry, but for safety sake I always keep the doors locked." The Explorer zoomed onto the crossroads, sending up a spray of muddy water.

Patsy kissed Billie's right hand which was at that very moment shifting into second. "I can't believe I'm here!" she said, puffing for breath, laughing, crying.

"I can." Billie said, smiling through teary eyes. She shifted up. Third. Fourth.

"But I really thought I had no choice, that you were destined to drive off without me."

"And then what would you have done? Spent the next 20 years secretly mourning? Pining at your old kitchen table, sipping brandy clandestinely, quietly weeping over a stray letter, poem or photograph?"

"Something like that," Patsy admitted. "Although it does sound pretty idiotic, when you put it that way. Still, what made you so sure of yourself?"

"Because our story is more than a mere parody of a heterosexual romance. Ours is a lesbian romance and a lesbian romance deserves a happy, if not particularly realistic, ending."

"Oh, Billie," Patsy said, "I don't care if we're unrealistic or not. I just know that I'll love you forever!"

So together, Patsy, Billie and Janeway (as well as Prince who, undetected, had squeezed into the spare tire well four days earlier) shifted into fifth gear.

The fog was lifting. Great possibilities lay ahead.

Acknowledgments

Many thanks to Tasha and Mary for allowing me to get up-close and personal with their Ford Explorer, to Paige Braddock for her terrific cover illustration, and to Carol for letting me to steal her jokes.